THE DON VASCO ROUTE

LUNWERG EDITORES

President
Juan Carlos Luna

Managing director
Jesús Infante

Managing director
Fernando Ondarza

Art director
Andrés Gamboa

Editorial coordination
Marta Papiol

Production director
Mercedes Carregal

Graphic design
Alejandra Gamboa

Text coordination
María José Moyano

ISBN: 978-84-9785-431-3

Legal deposit: B-50516-2007

LUNWERG EDITORES

Beethoven, 12 - 08021 BARCELONA - Tel. 93 201 59 33 - Fax 93 201 15 87

Luchana, 27 - 28010 MADRID - Tel. 91 593 00 58 - Fax 91 593 00 70

Callejón de la Rosa, 23. Tlacopac, San Ángel - 01060 MÉXICO, D.F. - Tel./Fax (52-55) 5662 5746

Printed in Spain

The Don Vasco Route

PHOTOGRAPHS

Adalberto Ríos Szalay

Ernesto Ríos Lanz

TEXTS

Silvia Figueroa Zamudio

Armando Mauricio Escobar Olmedo

Gerardo Sánchez Díaz

Igor Cerda Farías

J. Benedict Warren

J.Ricardo Aguilar González

Juan Carlos Cortés Máximo

Ricardo León Alanís

Michoacán
el alma de México

Michoacán
un gobierno diferente

LUNWERG
EDITORES

Michoacán experienced two crucial moments in the birth of mixed-race Mexico: the insensitive actions of Nuño de Guzmán and the arrival and settling of a man who brought the best of the Spanish humanist and Renaissance spirit: Vasco de Quiroga.

The importance of Quiroga's work is rooted in the fact that it goes beyond a mere importing of values, practices and conceptions; instead, he attempted to introduce new models through the most advanced social ideas of the age, in accordance with the culture and conditions of the indigenous peoples.

Vasco de Quiroga was not content with simply curbing excesses and arbitrary behaviour, nor did he believe in mass conversions. He did not accept the imposition of, or subjection to a culture; on the contrary, he believed in the abilities and the spirituality of all men and, in particular, of the *purepecha* people. He made sure that not only were they not subjugated, but that they learned and developed new cultural processes.

Quiroga was the founder of one of the first higher education institutions on the continent, and he introduced new methods of education and work training. He was also outstanding as a social worker, incorporating aspects of health, agricultural production, education, justice and communal support.

He was a lawyer who had a great capacity for bringing people together, as well as promoting dialogue and agreement between different cultures, both in Africa and in the multicultural sphere of Granada — experiences that helped to shape him as a universal man.

Vasco de Quiroga was a pioneer of hospitality, ensuring that each of his communities had places in which to receive and care for the people who were travelling our roads and paths. He also organised the indigenous communities in accordance with the specialisation of their skills: these include the lute-makers of Paracho, the lacquer work artists of Uruapan and the master coppersmiths of Santa Clara, all of whom are still producing their skilled work.

But especially, Vasco de Quiroga attempted to create a fairer society, given the opportunity that a New World represented. Quiroga sowed and reaped the acknowledgment of the Michoacan people, who awarded him the highest honour, and which has lasted for almost 500 years — the title of «Tata».

As a result of all the above, the government of Michoacán has decided to share the profound experience produced by coming into contact with the work, environment and feelings of an exceptional event in the history of humanity, through the development of an important model of cultural tourism.

Michoacán has designed the Don Vasco Route, which takes visitors on a journey through the diversity of local landscapes, the heritage constructed with a sense of community, encounters with creators who re-create secular works and spaces on a daily basis, the pleasures of a rich cuisine, and all within a region that is steeped in an ancient hospitality.

Michoacán invites you to travel the Don Vasco Route, to enjoy the places and experiences that encourage optimism in the finest values of humanity.

Lázaro Cárdenas Batel
Constitutional Governor
of the State of Michoacán

Nowadays, large waves of tourists are travelling the planet in search of knowledge and experience of different peoples and their cultures: values, traditions, ways of life, types and techniques of work. This kind of tourism is the preserve of more educated visitors, who try to make contact and interact with the inhabitants of the communities, to discover and enjoy their natural beauty and their historical-cultural heritage.

As Mexico is one of the six most exceptional countries in the world with the greatest biodiversity and cultural resources, in recent years the country has diversified its tourism policy, granting more importance to cultural tourism and nature tourism.

Within this context, Michoacán plays an important role, as it not only possesses countless natural resources and a valuable cultural heritage, but also because we have been working in recent years to map the cultural resources and improve the urban image of the communities that make up «The Space of Don Vasco». This project includes the revitalisation of architectural monuments, with the participation of civil society, celebrating international level cultural events, promoting our rich Michoacán cuisine and making every effort to improve the quality of the tourist services offered to visitors.

We are attempting to link these actions with a form of sustainable tourism through the project the Vasco de Quiroga Tourist Route, the aim of which is to promote our rich natural and cultural heritage in the Pátzcuaro Lake Area, the Purepecha Meseta and the Eleven Peoples Ravine.

The emblematic figure of the project is Vasco de Quiroga, the great humanist who, some 500 years ago, promoted a model of community coexistence based on equality, fraternity, justice and organised labour, all with a profound social sense and whose legacy – expressed through the teaching of arts and trades – is still very present in the communities.

Through the Don Vasco Route, the Department of Tourism of the Government of Michoacán seeks to contribute with a sustainable regional development, through the careful, responsible management of our natural resources and heritage.

In this way, visitors can enjoy the natural environment and take an active part in a living culture, re-created by our skilled artisans and our talented musicians and dancers, at the same time as they enjoy the aromas and flavours of the dishes prepared by our creative traditional chefs.

Genovevo Figueroa Zamudio
Minister of Tourism for the Government of the State of Michoacán

Index

THE VASCO DE QUIROGA ROUTE

Adalberto Ríos Szalay

With thanks to the maestro Medardo Mendez:
A great expert in his Purhepecha land and culture
and who, through his generous patience
and great friendship, has transmitted knowledge and
feelings that enabled me to evaluate the values
that distinguish the noble land of Michoacan.

Tourism —owing to the millions of human beings that work in it and the profits that it produces— is one of the most important areas of the world economy. But apart from the figures in monetary terms (and which have now surpassed those of the automobile and oil industries), the significance of tourism is also greater owing to its influence on society and culture.

The times are long past when tourism was merely limited to sunbathing and beaches; as well as rest and relaxation, travellers have now realised that leisure is a fuller, more satisfactory experience when it involves the spirit as well as the body.

Encounters with the natural setting and culture of the places people visit on holiday have given rise to the two most important elements in world tourism flows: ecotourism and cultural tourism. Both varieties require an approach that maximises visitors' enjoyment and the introduction of policies and mechanisms that ensure the organised, sustained and careful functioning of phenomena and environments that must be preserved and developed.

Given its interest in biodiversity and creative plurality, UNESCO has invited its member states to present proposals, like dialogue routes, that refer to periods in man's history which, beyond those of wartime and other painful events, have represented exchanges of cultural experiences, knowledge, values and goods through migration, trade and art.

Thus, the Silk Road, the slave route and the iron route could give rise to models of cultural tourism that promote community development, the preservation and recreation of people's heritage as well as satisfaction for travellers who have succeeded in enriching their minds.

When we travel nowadays to explore different natural settings, with their constructions built in accordance with the knowledge of the time, needs and circumstances, and especially when we come into contact with the heirs of these ecosystems and cultural practices, it all represents an experience that helps to clarify the reasons why man has travelled throughout history — to discover the world and to find out about other peoples.

The state of Michoacan has created the Vasco de Quiroga cultural tourism route, with the aim of sharing and promoting what was an exemplary human experience, one that is important not only for the history of the region, but for the whole nation. The central focus of this experience is the work of a humanist who was inspired by Renaissance thought, and who worked in a unique natural environment, in respectful interrelation with a virtuous people, in order to create a new world.

To this end, the Michoacan University of San Nicolas de Hidalgo, with the participation of renowned historians, has created a series of works on different aspects of the life and work of the man in question, as well as the cultural, social, economic and political effects of his work.

Taking into consideration the places where Quiroga worked, the variety of landscapes, the social models he designed (such as the Pueblo-Hospitals), the planning and founding of towns, the manual skills and trades he promoted, his work in education, his philosophy and links with the currents of thought of Renaissance and utopian authors, as well as the work continued by his followers, our experts in the tourism planning have designed a route that offers many different options to the traveller.

The route is comprised of eleven circuits that have been organised to ensure the permanent improvement of the services that tourism requires; these include the work done by transport companies, hotel owners, restaurant owners, travel agents, craftsmen and local authorities.

Travelling the Vasco de Quiroga Route is an experience that is pleasant, stimulating and educational; it is a way of travelling through history, and of following in the footsteps of an exceptional man who had great ambitions.

The Vasco de Quiroga Route covers the Purhepecha region, where he lived and worked, as well as neighbouring areas that help to complement the overall view and to facilitate the routes, through their service infrastructure.

Let us begin our journey by following the path that travellers take when arriving by road from the city of Mexico; they will know that they have arrived in Michoacan when they see the Los Azufres mountains exhaling steam and, further on, when they see the vaporous veil that often conceals the mountains, it is their first sighting of the land of fishermen and lakes— Cuitzeo, as the Aztecs used to call it.

The main feature of Cuitzeo, which lies on the banks of the lake of the same name (and is the second largest in Mexico) is the Augustine monumental monastery of Santa Maria Magdalena, which has a church with one of the most beautiful plateresque façades in Mexico —and is now more beautiful than ever, thanks to the painstaking restoration carried out by the Morelia section of the active civil society group «Adopt a Work of Art".

On entering the monastery, the visitor feels as if he has been immersed in the medieval age, surrounded by sights such as the cloister which is protected by fantastic gargoyles, the marvellous fresco paintings, the pilgrims' gateway, the open chapel and the chapterhouse decorated with sacred motifs and elaborate geometric designs which bear a strong resemblance to the work of avant-garde artists.

Meanwhile, the monastery library represents an important item of Augustine bibliographic heritage. It is also the home of the Museum of *Estampas* (religious illustrations) and part of its newly-gained space will be set aside for research work.

Owing to its urban layout and valuable monuments, Cuitzeo has been included on the list of Magical Towns devised by the Department of Federal Tourism. This list groups together towns of exceptional value and charm, and whose inhabitants and local authorities are committed to preserving and constantly developing their patrimonial heritage.

Cuitzeo lies only 34 kilometres from Morelia, the capital of Michoacan.

Morelia is Michoacan's main reception and distribution centre for national and international tourism. It belongs to the select group of cities throughout the world that are deemed to be items of World Heritage. The capital is the home of the Michoacan University of San Nicolas de Hidalgo, which is a continuation of the College of St. Nicholas, founded by Vasco de Quiroga. Among the treasures conserved in its cathedral are the walking stick and Episcopal hat of the man who became the first Bishop of Michoacan.

Vasco de Quiroga's legacy is present on many murals and paintings on buildings in the state capital, and he is also portrayed on the stained-glass window in the cathedral.

As Morelia is the starting point for the Vasco de Quiroga Route, it gives visitors the opportunity to discover one of the most beautiful cities on the American continent. The city that used to be known as Valladolid has 1,400 buildings and monumental constructions listed in its historical centre, including the churches of St. Francis, Mercy and the Nuns, as well as the palaces of justice, government and the municipality.

Other outstanding features include the cathedral (the tallest Baroque building of its style on the continent), the aqueduct, the church of Las Rosas, with its extraordinary altarpieces — it was also an important part of the first conservatory in America — and the stunning Clavijero palace, which was one of the most important Jesuit colleges in Mexico.

One way of gauging the spirit of the city is to go on a walk, starting from the Fountain of las Tarascas, one of the city's icons. Stroll down Fray Antonio de San Miguel Street, a pedestrian-only thoroughfare which has the advantage of the cool shade provided by its trees, while visitors feel like a rest, they can sit down on one of the long lines of benches that flank the street.

On both sides of the street stand ancient mansions, and if you peer through their elaborate wrought iron gates, you can see courtyards that are reminiscent of old Seville.

Another pleasant detail is the fact that the street runs almost parallel to the neighbouring aqueduct, which gives one the sense of going back in time — thanks to the buildings and constructions and the peace that they exhale —to an ordinary day in the 18th or 19th centuries, just like the scenes represented in the paintings in the Regional Museum.

The street ends just in front of the church of Guadalupe, perhaps the last Baroque work in Mexico. Its profuse ornamentation, which brings together many different popular styles, is more than enough reason for the traveller to stop and gaze at it for a few minutes, to appreciate its floral motifs and the other merely decorative flourishes, which can only be compared with those of its sister church at Tlalpujahua.

Morelia has wide doorways where people, conversation and rumours tend to come together and flow. The city also has numerous squares, beginning with the two that flank the cathedral.

At Plaza Valladolid, where the city was founded, visitors can take a look in the Casa de la Artesanías (The House of Traditional Crafts), which includes examples of Michoacan popular art, one of the most important styles in Mexico.

The old monastery of Carmen is the home of the dynamic Casa de la Cultura, where interest in the arts has breathed new life into a beautiful space. One of the most outstanding features of the building is its trilogy of domes, each of which was built in a different century, and can all be seen clearly from the neighbouring Gardens of Carmen.

Morelia has a large number of museums, including the Regional History Museum, the Colonial Art Museum, the Modern Art Museum and the Museum of *Dulces* (sweets and candies). Meanwhile, the Art Gallery that has opened in the old monastery of St. Augustine is particularly worthy of mention.

Morelia is the site for a range of international festivals dedicated to music (such as the organ and the guitar festival) and cinema, as well as international chess and golf tournaments.

After sunset, visitors can enjoy the spectacle resulting from the fact that more and more buildings are now illuminated, giving different attractive views of the city. Meanwhile, on Saturdays and official holidays, visitors can also enjoy the nocturnal spectacle of light, music and fireworks at the cathedral.

Before continuing on the Vasco de Quiroga Route, we should stop to reflect upon the city's character. It is a Spanish city in America that was not built on top of any pre-Hispanic settlement; it was born out of a sense of innovation, with an undeniable Castilian touch. Its original name was Valladolid, and in the garden of Las Rosas there are statues that pay homage to two of the gentlemsn who came to form part of the heritage of this new mixed-race nation: Miguel Cervantes de Saavedra and Vasco de Quiroga.

It is now time for us to head off for the land that called out to Vasco de Quiroga —to the region on which the great humanist focused the best of his ideas and actions. It was an area that he devotedly referred to as «my beloved wife", and it represents the fundamental part of our route — Purhepecha territory, Indian Mexico.

The nucleus or heart of the Vasco de Quiroga Route covers 15 municipalities and 40 communities that are home to 63% of the indigenous population of Michoacan. It spans three geographical regions that have a very rich biodiversity, the Lake Region of Pátzcuaro, the Purhepecha Meseta, the Canyon of the Eleven Peoples and which are also the location for the main populations belonging to the Purhepecha culture.

THE LAKE REGION

No sooner have we left Morelia behind than the tower of the monastery of Tiripetio appears in the middle of the rural landscape; this building was once home to one of the first higher education institutions on the continent.

Tiripetio acted as a centre for Augustinian studies, and enjoyed the protection and enthusiasm of Vasco de Quiroga. He developed a comprehensive educational project that went from the schooling of small children to the training of master craftsmen — the same carpenters, locksmiths, cobblers, blacksmiths, dyers and tailors who, once they had learned their trades, went on to become promoters and teachers of their skills in other towns.

Tiripetio was the first place on the continent in which higher education was made available. Subjects included those of the arts and theology, and with syllabuses that had similar content to as those of European universities. Another priority task was the study of indigenous languages.

One student who did brilliantly in his studies in Tiripetio was Huitzimengari, the son of the last Purhepecha king; he studied Latin and some Greek and Hebrew.

One important feature of the Pátzcuaro Route is the small town of Tupataro, the chapel of which possesses an exceptional gem of Neo Hispanic art — in addition to its Baroque altarpiece, it also has an altar fron-

Fragment of Juan O'Gorman's mural History of Michoacán, Gertrudis Bocanegra Library, Patzcuaro.

tispiece made from corn stalk paste. It is a unique work in its genre, as is its coffering, exquisitely decorated with the skill of the indigenous people, and which incorporates both forms and colours as well as little details, such as the dog chewing on a bone beneath the table of the Last Supper.

Nearby Tupataro lies the community of Cuanajo, a town abounding in skilled craftsmen who manufacture wooden furniture that is carved and decorated in their own special style.

Pátzcuaro is one of the fundamental centres of the Vasco de Quiroga Route. As it was considered to be an ideal spot, on the shores of the eponymous lake, Vasco de Quiroga chose it to be the main location for his work. It was here that he founded the College of St. Nicholas, now the Museum of Popular Arts, a place that reveals the simple yet functional nature of Quiroga's project. Inside the building visitors can see the vestiges of a pre-Hispanic plinth and a curious decorative feature in the form of cattle vertebra in the dwellings.

The basilica of Our Lady of Health is a building that was constructed by Vasco de Quiroga on an elevated spot that presides over the city. The original design was for an enormous cathedral.

One of the outstanding features in the basilica is the image of the Virgin, made from corn stalk paste by the indigenous maestros, according to Quiro-

ga's instructions. As a result of this sacred image, the basilica is an important place of worship, as well as for the fact that this was the final resting place for Quiroga's remains.

Vasco de Quiroga's inventiveness had a determining influence on the urban layout of Pátzcuaro — note, for example, the dimensions of the main square where, unlike most other Mexican towns, there are no religious buildings, only civil ones.

Very near to what is now known as Plaza Vasco de Quiroga (and preceded by a statue and fountain dedicated to him), there are a number of important monuments, such as the unusual House of the Eleven Courtyards, an old monastery that has now become a complex of workshops and shops selling magnificent works of popular art.

Other outstanding features include the college and church of the Jesuits, an order which, given its importance with respect to education, was supported by Vasco de Quiroga. Meanwhile, just in front of the order's headquarters stands El Sagrario with its singular atrial wall.

The Gertrudis Bocanegra public library contains an important mural portraying Michoacan history, painted by the renowned Mexican artist Juan O'Gorman between 1941 and 1942. The central figure of the work is Vasco de

Quiroga, accompanied by Thomas More, the author of *Utopia*. The mural is a didactic piece in which figures from different ages appear in a colourful work that represents a virtuoso, comprehensive history lesson.

Owing to its many attributes, Pátzcuaro forms part of the Department of Federal Tourism's Magic Towns program. The town makes an excellent base for visiting neighbouring towns linked with the life and work of Quiroga, as well as for travelling the lake circuit and the tour of the lake's islands.

Tzintzuntzan is an onomatopoeic name deriving from the buzzing produced by the many hummingbirds that can be found in this spot. It was the capital city for Purhepecha nobility, as can be seen from the *yacatas*, or ceremonial plinths in its archaeological area, as well as various pieces on display in the site's museum.

It was in Tzintzuntzan that Vasco de Quiroga was invested as the first Bishop of Michoacan in 1538. The town contains a monumental Franciscan monastery built between the 15th and 17th centuries. The building has undergone an exhaustive restoration process that involved the young people of the town. The cloister features Mudejar decorative elements as well as the remains of frescoes.

One outstanding feature is its open chapel and the dramatic presence of the ancient olive trees that were planted by Vasco de Quiroga. One only has to walk through this enormous cloister to feel the creative energy that was set in motion during those early years of the viceroyship. An ingenious monument dedicated to the first bishop shows the affection the town's inhabitants have for him.

Tzintzuntzan has a craft market offering items made from a fabric called *chuspata*, and which is woven from plant fibres from the lake. The market also contains several masonry and pottery workshops.

Santa Fe de la Laguna is a key element in the history of Vasco de Quiroga. It was there that, in 1533, he founded the first Pueblo-Hospital of Michoacan. A community museum in the original building displays some of the personal belongings of this man whose presence and energy made such a difference to this place.

Inhabitants of Santa Fe speak of Vasco de Quiroga in the present tense, and the place that he built to welcome and care for pilgrims and the sick, and to give the local people education, meetings and evangelisation, still exists as the town's nucleus and meeting point. This achievement is a clear tribute to the personality of a man who combined kindness with an unshakeable will of iron.

The presence of women in the Pueblo-Hospital, the church and the square in which his statue stands emphasises the importance that the participation of women had in his project.

Anyone wishing to learn more about the life of the nearby communities and to enjoy the beauty of Lake Pátzcuaro — which has inspired both symphonies and love songs — should travel the scenic route. This takes the visitor to Ihuatzio, a place abounding in coyotes, and where there is also an archaeological site. The family homes made out of adobe and red tiles, with their fishing nets stretched out across their gardens, can be seen as far as the communities of Ucazanastacua and Tarerio. These two places are famed for their cuisine, which features fish such as *charales*, *acumaras*, carp and, of course, the highly-prized whitefish.

Even though archipelagos are normally associated with seas and oceans, Pátzcuaro, one of Michoacan's inland seas, has its own archipelago made up of islands with beautiful names: the smallest is called Tecuena, which means «good honey»; others include Yunuén («half moon»), Pacanda («pushing something in the water»), Janitzio («hair of corn»), Uranden («flat-bottomed boat»), and Jarácuaro, which is no longer an island, and is dedicated to a lunar deity.

If you take the motorboat trip, you can enjoy the aquatic choreography of the fishermen of Janitzio, as they demonstrate the ancient art of fishing with butterfly nets.

Travellers can spend the night on Yunuén in beautiful wooden *trojes* — the traditional Purhepecha dwelling — or on Pacanda, in an old building that has been painstakingly restored.

After Pátzcuaro, visitors can take the traditional crafts circuit, which includes Santa Clara del Cobre, where Vasco de Quiroga — that great promoter of work for utilitarian ends — is remembered with the cooking pots in which they make their renowned *carnitas*, or meat dishes. The skill and dexterity of these craftsmen in hammering, embossing, engraving, silver plating and enamelling led to the creation of new objects such as trays, serving dishes, vases and simple decorative pieces that have garnered great praise in national and international competitions.

Zirahuén is a beautiful lake with limpid water, surrounded by pine forests where, in harmony with nature, cabins have been built with all modern conveniences. Together with the restaurants that serve regional cuisine, these represent yet another attraction for the area.

THE PURHEPECHA MESETA

Uruapan is the second most important city in the state; it is the gateway to the Purhepecha Meseta and is considered to be the world avocado capital, owing to the volume and quality of the crops produced here.

Uruapan enjoys an exceptional climate and flora, and this explains why it has the only urban national park in Mexico within its city limits. The park stretches over 898,000 square metres of lush land that begins at the spring known as the Devil's Knee; this is the source of the crystalline Cupatitzio («the singing river»), which runs through the prodigious greenery accompanied by the calls of many different kinds of birds.

Walking along the paths that weave between the river and the fountains created by artists who emulate and pay tribute to water is a stimulating exercise, and a great opportunity for the enjoyment of the senses.

A fundamental example of Quiroga's work can be found in Uruapan — the Pueblo-Hospital that was built in 1534 on the foundations of a pre-Hispanic ceremonial centre. The city grew and developed from that original nucleus.

The Pueblo-Hospital of Uruapan was one of the first of its kind in America — a meeting place for travellers, for people who came to study and learn, for sick people and for those who came simply to be heard. It was one of the crucibles of Mexican-Spanish miscegenation.

Its wide corridors, its arches, columns, beams and roof are reminiscent of Castille, but a closer look produces a surprise — the same surprise that the monks must have felt — when one realises that the indigenous people who took part in the project were active co-creators, from the very beginning. Discovering and recognising that talent was the starting point of Vasco de Quiroga's work.

The elegant sobriety of the Pueblo-Hospital of Uruapan has three exquisite features that should be highlighted: its filigreed windows, the façade of the chapel of the Holy Sepulchre and the frescoes in the latter. The stonework includes elements of the plateresque, Mudejar touches and others of an unquestionable indigenous style — a mixture that symbolises the meeting of cultures that took place at that time, and particularly the work of Vasco de Quiroga.

The Pueblo-Hospital continues to be a meeting place, in accordance with the Quirogan spirit. Every year, on Palm Sunday, the Tianguis Craftwork festival is held. It is the largest popular art event on the continent, and brings together maestros from the fields of stonework, jewellery, ceramics, cabinetmaking, instrument-making, basket-making, fabrics and metalwork.

Vasco de Quiroga is said to have died in one of these halls — the one that is now a museum dedicated to the popular arts that he worked so hard to promote. Another person who is also said to have passed away here is Brother Juan de San Miguel — a figure closely linked with Quiroga's life and work.

Uruapan is the starting point for the path that leads up to the Purhepecha Meseta, which begins at San Lorenzo, a small town whose old hospital and church are relatively well conserved, as well as its atrium with its masonry cross.

The path then goes up to Angahuan, which means «the place after the slope". This is a community predominated by the Purhepecha language and culture, and is expressed in their clothing, fabrics and rich cuisine. In the heart of the town lies the old Quiroga hospital, while next door stands the church with its extraordinary façade carved out of pink stone, featuring Mudejar elements and a relief design of the Apostle St. James the Great.

Angahuan's contemporary history cannot be separated from Parícutin, the volcano that first erupted in 1943 right next to the neighbouring town of Parangaicutiro. Angahuan is a kind of balcony from where visitors can look down on the massive lava flow, nascent forest and the tower that is completely surrounded by volcanic rock — the only construction to have survived the eruption.

In Angahuan there is a comfortable refuge where visitors can spend the night. It offers good food and hires out horses for going on trips to the volcanic area. There is a tourist route around Parícutin that enables visitors to go and see the remains of the church tower surrounded by lava, and to see how — millimetre by millimetre — nature is taking over the area again. Furthermore, visitors can discover the spot where the renowned Mexican volcanologist and painter Dr. Atl set up camp, in order to create a pictorial testimony of the amazing phenomenon that stunned Mexico and the rest of the world.

Further along the Purhepecha Meseta path lies Charapan, a town that was founded in 1532, and where some of the dwellings where the people live and stored their highly-prized corn have survived to the present day.

These houses are all made out of woods, held together without using one single nail. They are comprised of beams, wall boards and fine strips of roofing boards.

Charapan also has a 17th century chapel and church.

In addition, the Purhepecha Meseta features the Chapels Circuit, a route that runs through the towns of Pomacuaran, Nurio, Cocucho and Zacán. These churches all have one common characteristic — their magnificent wooden roofs, which resemble a kind of gigantic upside-down wooden trays which, in the case of Michoacan, eschew the Mudejar style of decoration (based on geometric figures) to give free rein to the indigenous styles, particularly the use of the flat wooden surfaces as «canvases" for storytelling through painting. These include the Passion of Christ in Tupátaro and the Litany of the Rosary in Zacán. As a result, they are jointly known as «ceilings with stories".

Every October in Zacán they hold the Purhepecha art competition, which brings thousands of people from different communities who show their skill at dancing, singing, musical performance and composition, featuring both traditional pieces and contemporary ones. This event is a multitudinous example of the cultural energy of the Purhepecha people.

The Caltzontzin dam, San Juan Nuevo and San Salvador Combutzio also form part of this circuit, which is characterised by its beautiful conifer forest settings.

The most important location in the Meseta's traditional crafts circuit is Paracho, a famous town of luthiers and guitarists, and which produces such excellent instruments that the town has achieved world recognition. Furthermore, it is yet another place where the memory of Tata Vasco (as Vasco de Quiroga is affectionately known in this region) still persists.

The last stop on the circuit is the Canyon of the Eleven Peoples, which includes Tangancícuaro and its beautiful lake Camécuaro, as well as the indigenous communities of Acachuén, Santo Tomás, Ichán and Carapan. In these towns, visitors can enjoy the tasty regional cuisine, browse through the attractive ceramic stalls and the cross-point embroidery and, with a little luck (given the frequency of local festivals) enjoy the cheerful Purhepecha music, which tends to feature pipe bands.

The project of the Vasco de Quiroga Route has the fundamental aim of inviting visitors to share the culture we have inherited, through quality services which help to benefit the communities.

Generating employment so as to offer tasty food, charming places to spend the night, good transport and the hospitality that Vasco de Quiroga promoted with his Pueblo-Hospitals — this is the best way to bring such a project to life, one that celebrates the vision of a man who recognised the dignity and talents of the original peoples of America.

VASCO DE QUIROGA
AND HOPE FOR THE FUTURE

Gerardo Sánchez Díaz
Historical Research Institute
University of Michoacán

Between Salamanca and Arévalo, in the heart of the Castilian *meseta*, in the middle of fields covered with golden wheat, crossed every so often by flocks of sheep and a landscape surrounded by hills covered with groves of Holm oaks, stands the Villa de Madrigal de las Altas Torres, which was founded in mediaeval times; its walls, eaten away by time, bear witness to the passing of centuries coloured by the events of old Spain. From far away, travelling along old, dusty roads, one can see its silhouette in the distance: it is made up of a large manor house on a slope above which projects the tower of the old church of St. Nicholas the Bishop, the patron saint of the town. As you walk along its streets, you realise the typical characteristics of its buildings, with their thick adobe and stone walls with tiled roofs that sometimes jut out into the street in the form of eaves, which afford pedestrians protection from the rain or the heat of the sun. The town's outline is visible from a long way off, «and the most eye-catching feature in the town is the church of St. Nicholas and the walls that surround the structure. The decay of the villa... contrasts with the vestiges that are still visible from better days, especially from when it was, at one time, the seat of the Castilian court».

As you walk its streets, most of which are cobbled, you see realise that the great importance that the town had, from the coats of arms of the many noble families that inhabited it over the years, including the shields of the Samaniegos and of the Quiroga family. «Many of those old buildings still stand, such as the palace where King Juan II of Castille lived with his first wife Doña Maria of Aragon, and where the renowned queen Isabel the Catholic was born to the king's second wife, Isabel of Portugal».

Madrigal now only possesses the remains of what used to be the Quiroga house, a building that was redolent of the family's nobility, and which was — in the late 15th century — inhabited by Vasco Vázquez de Quiroga, a native of the province of Lugo, and his wife Maria Alonso de la Cárcel, who was from Arévalo in Avila province. They gave birth to Álvaro, the father of Gaspar de Quiroga, who would become the Cardinal Primate of Spain and the Inquisitor General; Álvaro was also father to Constanza, who became a nun in the Augustine Convent of Our Lady of Grace in Madrigal, and Vasco, the future first Bishop of Michoacán.

Quiroga's biographers differ on the year of his birth: some say he was born in 1478, others in 1479, but the most accepted version is that he was born in 1470. Even though no certificate has survived, his birthday is traditionally given as 3rd February. His life as a child and an adolescent must have been played out in the peace and quiet of the town of Madrigal, after which he left for the University of Salamanca to study law. Little is known of this stage of his life, and his biographers do not pick up his history again until 1525 and 1526, when he was already practising (according to Dr. Benedict Warren's studies) as a judge in the courts of Orán, in North Africa. This overseas posting gave Quiroga his first chance to observe the cultural differences between the Muslim world and Western Christian tradition to which he belonged. The same historical study also informs us of the role that Vasco de Quiroga played in the diplomatic field when, on behalf of the Spanish Crown, he participated in the negotiations and peace treaty between the Spanish monarchy and the Muslim kingdom of Tremecén. Thus, «Quiroga's work in Orán was, in many ways, a preparation for the type of work he would carry out on a larger scale in the New World. Orán was a recently conquered colony, and was still in an unstable condition, which meant that relations between conquerors and conquered were less than satisfactory. His work there consisted of investigating the injustices of an official previously sent by the Crown, whose administration had brought complaints from several groups in the colony. He was also working in a region in which most of the people did not possess a Hispanic culture and education. He would encounter these same problems in Nueva España, even though with greater scope and basic importance, and he would attempt to solve them with the same careful attention to the strict requirements of the law».

At the end of the first decade of colonial dominance in Mexico, we find Vasco de Quiroga forming part of the Second *Audiencia* [court], the aim of which was to investigate the excesses of the First *Audiencia*, and especially those of the notorious Nuño de Guzmán, about whom the Spanish Crown had received countless complaints of the murder, outrage and theft that he had perpetrated on the native people; some of these complaints were even from Spaniards — especially members of the clergy — who were opposed to Guzmán's thieving ambitions. On his arrival in Nueva España, Quiroga found a disheartening social panorama, brought about by the splintering of the old Middle American political and social structures following the war of conquest and the imposition of the colonial system. On the streets of Mexico City, as well as in Tzintzuntzan, Quiroga saw starvation and poverty. He saw many Indians rifling through the rubbish to find scraps of food with which to sate their hunger. In the face of this devastating situation, Quiroga proposed to find an answer to the problems, and he did so by reading the social theories of Thomas More, the well-known English humanist. More's theories inspired his project to set up the Pueblo-Hospitals of Santa Fe in Mexico and Santa Fe de la Laguna in Michoacán, as meeting places for aid and offer Christian charity to the needy, based on a new model of coexistence in which religious practices and productive work were interwoven, together with education and physical rest.

Meanwhile, Quiroga brought the full force of the law to bear on a number of greedy Spaniards, especially the *encomenderos* [colonial farmers], who only viewed the natives of the land as instruments for their own enrichment, even if the land became soaked in blood. For several decades Quiroga continued a protracted lawsuit against the *encomendero* Juan Infante over the ownership of the land at Uayameo, where Quiroga had built his Pueblo-Hospital of Santa Fe de la Laguna. He continued this legal dispute later on as the first Bishop of Michoacán, and on more than one occasion he was heard to declare before notaries that he would rather lose his post of prelate and his own life than allow the *encomendero* Infante to gain possession of the lands on which Quiroga was building his model of social reorganisation: the Pueblo-Hospital de Santa Fe, the institution that later helped to finance another of his great projects in the Michoacán area: the Royal College of St. Nicholas the Bishop, which was founded in Pátzcuaro, and was the school where future priests were educated, and who would be responsible for administrating the sacrament in his diocese, as well as helping to promote the new cultural model.

Quiroga's defence of the rights of indigenous people — both lakeside dwellers and mountain people such as those of Michoacán — developed with the passing of time into what became known as the Quirogian indigenous tradition. This tradition later turned into worship and a form of identity for the indigenous peoples, centuries even after Quiroga's death. This phenomenon was witnessed by the Jesuit historian Francisco Xavier Clavijero, during his stay in Michoacán between 1763 and 1765. Speaking of Vasco de Quiroga, Clavijero says that at that time he noticed that «this famous prelate, who can be compared with the first fathers of Christianity, did infinite work to help the people of Michoacán, instructing them as an apostle and loving them as a father; he built churches, founded hospitals and encouraged each Indian settlement to specialise in a particular field of trade, so that their reciprocal dependence would keep them united with the links of charity, and thus they would perfect their art, and nobody would be without the means to live. The memory of all these benefits is still alive in the minds of the natives so many centuries later, as if they were still experiencing his good works. The first thing that Indian women do, when their children are old enough to understand, is to speak to them of «Tata Vasco» (which is their name for him, owing to their filial love for him), telling them all the things he did for their nation, and showing the children his portrait and teaching them never to pass before it without kneeling».

Thus, the figure of Vasco de Quiroga became a moral support for the survival of the identity of all the people of Michoacán, especially those that had anything to do with Quiroga's two main foundations, the Pueblo-Hospital de Santa Fe and the College of St. Nicholas. In the mid-18th century, when the existence of the College of St. Nicholas was endangered by a new diocesan institution represented by the Seminary College of Valladolid, Juan José Moreno, the then-rector of the College of St. Nicholas, evoked the figure of Vasco de Quiroga in his defence of the pre-eminence of the College of St. Nicholas, and to this end he wrote his famous book *Fragments of the Life and Virtues of the Illustrious and Reverend Gentleman Vasco de Quiroga, first Bishop of the Holy Church-Cathedral of Michoacán and founder of the Royal and Original College of St. Nicholas the Bishop of Valladolid*. In this work, he interweaves two stories — those of Vasco de Quiroga and of the College of St. Nicholas — into one single whole. At that time nobody would dare to profane the memory of the first Bishop by relegating the institution he created, to which he had ceded his spiritual legacy and his material assets. This first biography of Vasco de Quiroga and the first history of the College became a protective shield for the institution, and ensured its survival.

In the past century, much has been written about Vasco de Quiroga's life and work in the Michoacán region. Hundreds of articles, leaflets, books and degree theses have been published about the nature, foundations and works of the first Bishop of Michoacán and which, thanks to a bibliographic essay compiled by Dr. Silvio Zavala (a consummate *Quirogist* from the 20th century), we now know everything that has been printed and published (in many languages apart from Spanish, including English, French, German, Portuguese and Russian) about Vasco de Quiroga, as well as about the region of Michoacán, and especially Pátzcuaro which Quiroga loved so much and where he now rests in

Fragments of the Life and Virtues of the Illustrious and Reverend Gentleman Vasco de Quiroga,

peace. Quiroga was a Quixote of Renaissance utopias, and came up with ideas that are still in the process of development, in spite of the models imposed by modernism and globalisation which are lacking in humanitarian principles.

In conclusion, I would like to quote that great educator of Mexican youth Miguel Arroyo de la Parra; 50 years ago, in a message entitled *Don Vasco de Quiroga calls us to the struggle*, he wrote: «Vasco de Quiroga, in all and with his Episcopal support, belongs to our people; he belongs to the future. In the same way that Hidalgo, with his full-length suit and his Guadalupe banner, rising up against the colonial past, is the symbol of Mexico and has nothing in common with those who excommunicated him and abominated him, or those opportunists who today hold *te deums* in homage to him. Quiroga, viewed in a strictly historical sense, is the opposite of the easy-going, accommodating approach; he belongs completely to those who are now fighting to make way for the dawn, to clear the path for a society that is based on col-

Town walls of Madrigal de las Altas Torres.

lective ownership of the means of production and where, therefore, once the causes of social injustice have been erased, the Indian and the negro will be equal to the white man and the half-caste, not only before the solemn word of law, but also in the simple reality of everyday life. Rather than marbles and bronzes, Vasco de Quiroga calls on us to persevere in the execution of those tasks which he began.

With the strength of his action and his thoughts, Vasco de Quiroga calls upon us today to fight in defence of the indigenous peoples of Mexico; to break the political shackles that prevent their democratic development, to destroy the economic inequalities that cause their hunger and poverty, so that they are no longer considered lesser or incapable, or as people in need of protection or tutelage. Instead, that they rise up in the full enjoyment of their dignity as men, to help them to develop a people's culture that is national in form, and modern and advanced in its content".

Wheatfields around
Madrigal de las Altas Torres.

Plaza de Isabel La Católica, Madrigal de las Altas Torres.

Church of St. Nicholas of Bari,
Madrigal de las Altas Torres.

*Main door of the old palace of
the Marquess of Castellanos,
Madrigal de las Altas Torres.*

The baptismal font where both
Isabel «the Catholic» and Vasco
de Quiroga were baptised.

Coffering in the church
of St. Nicholas of Bari,
Madrigal de las Altas Torres.

THE LAWYER VASCO DE QUIROGA, RESIDENT MAGISTRATE IN ORÁN

1525-1526

J. Benedict Warren
Historical Research Institute
University of Michoacán

When Vasco de Quiroga arrived in the New World, he was already well on in years, almost elderly, with many years of experience in the service of the Crown of Castille. However, we have been unable to discover much about his life during those important years. The Simancas Archive in Spain contains some documents that shed a little light on his work as a servant of the king for a year and a half, from March 1525 to September 1526. With respect to Quiroga's subsequent life, we must remember that during this period he was not working in Spain, but in the city of Orán and its surrounding area, a recently conquered colony on the Mediterranean coast of Africa. Orán is located in the western part of what is now Algeria, but at the time that Quiroga was there, the region that now makes up Algeria was divided up into several different Muslim kingdoms. Orán is not far from Spain; almost directly to the north, on the other side of a relatively narrow strip of the Mediterranean lies the Spanish city of Cartagena.

The conquest of Orán represented an extension of the Christian Reconquest of Spain, a struggle that had lasted more than seven centuries. After the Catholic Monarchs Ferdinand and Isabel had conquered the last Moorish kingdom in the Iberian Peninsula (Granada, in 1492), they decided to continue pushing the Arabs back in the north of Africa. King Ferdinand was always hopeful about the Crusades, and that they would retake Jerusalem. One of the few positive results of this new Crusade was the seizing of Orán, which fell to Spanish forces in 1509.

When Quiroga arrived in Orán as a visiting magistrate in 1525, Spanish domination had only lasted for 16 years, and the colony was already beset with problems. In order to understand the situation, one must bear in mind that for many centuries, the city had been a trade centre where European merchants had done business with traders from the northwest of Africa. Merchants from France and the various kingdoms of the Italian and Iberian peninsulas would bring their fabrics, glassware and ironwork and return with tanned hides, ivory, gold, iron weapons and slaves. As a result, the city had a very international population, with Muslims from Africa and exiles from Spain as well as Jews, Savoyards, Genoese, Neapolitans, French, Catalans, Valencians and Castilians. This rather cosmopolitan situation resulted in conflict.

The problems that led the Spanish Crown to send the lawyer Quiroga to Orán arose from the activities of the city mayor, the lawyer Alonso Páez de Ribera. The mayor was the person who most directly represented the power of the Crown of Castille in the new territory, which he governed on behalf of the king. It appears that Alonso Páez de Ribera took up his position in 1520, but he had a lot of problems. In 1522, he wrote a report to the Crown on the lack of safety at the beach of Orán and in the town of Mazalquivir (or Mersel-Kebir, as it was better known in Arabic). In that same year, Páez de Ribera returned to the court in Spain for a certain time, leaving his wife in charge of the problems in Orán. He informed the Crown that he and his wife had had to seize food and clothes from the Christian, Moorish and Jewish merchants so as to distribute the goods among the Spanish troops who were suffering from hunger and cold. He requested that the soldiers be paid their salaries so

they could pay off the merchants. Meanwhile, the Crown had also received complaints from the other authorities in Orán (both military and civil) about the mayor's activities. On 21st April 1523, the city councillors wrote a letter to the Crown claiming that Páez de Ribera had caused harm to many people during the almost three years in which he had run the city. He had taken a large amount of money from the merchants and traders, Jews, Moors and Christians, in the form of loans and through other unfair, illegal measures. As he was still away from the city, the councillors requested that he return in order that he be confined to his dwelling.

Meanwhile, a group of army officers had also send a request complaining that the mayor had arrested and tried the leader of the rural people in the city of Orán. The mayor had accused him of selling a horse to the Moors and of having harboured one of them. The mayor had imprisoned the captain without sentence or bail for two months. Generally speaking, the situation was similar to the one that Quiroga would have to deal with later on in Nueva España with Nuño de Guzmán.

On 3rd October 1523, King Carlos I signed, in Logroño, a warrant for the appointment of a resident magistrate in Orán. The magistrate was warned that an inspection would be carried out on the fraud perpetrated by army officers who had included disabled and absent men in their records as well as their servants and friends, who received salaries in the form of clothing and ammunition. Payments had also been received for soldiers who were absent, dead or taken captive. Furthermore, the resident magistrate would have to check the reports by captains and officers on all paid by the Crown. He would also have to look into possible transgressions by the mayor and other officials.

However, this warrant took a long time to take effect; Páez de Ribera's lieutenant was still in his post in November 1524. The first record to be found referring to Vasco de Quiroga's activities as resident magistrate to the mayor of Orán is dated 6th March 1525. Unfortunately, the transcription of the residence trial, if it still exists in some archive in Spain, has not come to light, and thus we do not know the exact date when Quiroga took up his position. But 6th March 1525 was the date of the issuing of a lawsuit submitted before Quiroga by two Savoyard merchants, Glaudio Bundilión and Tomás Bretón, who claimed that Páez de Ribera had confiscated 85 bolts of fabric from them. They claimed the goods were worth 5,625 doubloons, though they were claiming a further 5,000 doubloons for losses resulting from said confiscation. They requested that the mayor should pay bail or be placed in custody. Quiroga granted their request, and imprisoned Páez de Ribera, first in the house where he himself was living, and afterwards, for greater security, in a hall in Razalcázar castle, though the mayor was free within the limitations of his imprisonment to take all necessary steps for the defence of his rights. Páez de Ribera appointed his lieutenant Liminiana as his defence lawyer. The case continued throughout the summer of 1525, while, no doubt, other cases were being dealt with by the magistrate. Páez de Ribera claimed in his defence that he had taken the bolts of fabric to help King Muley Abdula of Tenez, who was a refugee in Orán, though he was still at war with the King of Tremecén (Tlemcen).

Finally, on 16th August, Quiroga found in favour of Bundilión and Bretón, and decreed that Páez de Ribera should give back the rolls of fabric or pay 60 Moorish gold doubloons for each roll. He also sentenced the defendant to pay 2,900 doubloons to the merchants to cover interest and losses. Páez de Ribera was also ordered to pay the costs of the trial. However, Páez de Ribera had protected himself. At the beginning of the residence, he had requested and received a royal warrant that enabled him to appeal against any large scale sentence that might be imposed upon him. He presented this warrant before Quiroga on 2nd September of that same year, and Quiroga was forced to grant him the appeal, the result of which is unknown. Thus in this case, Quiroga protected the legal interests of the merchants, even though they were not Castilian and even though the judge had presented arguments for the good of the state to justify the confiscation of the goods.

Another brief but complicated lawsuit during Quiroga's activities in Orán involved a wealthy Genoese called Baptista Caxines. He was a hatter with a workshop that employed more than 10 people. A tailor called Alexos de Pastrana also lived in the city with his wife María de Garay. At some point during the Páez de Ribera case, Caxines had made an agreement with Pastrana – as Caxines explained it, Pastrana had allowed him to have sexual access to his wife when the former desired.

In October 1524, the case had been brought before the lawyer Liminiana (Páez de Ribera's lieutenant) who had placed Caxines in prison and, on 24th November of that same year, sentenced him to pay a fine of 24 ducats to the royal chamber and to carry out repairs to government buildings. In March 1525, Caxines appealed against the decision before Quiroga and in November Quiroga revoked the previous decision, not because he judged Caxines to be innocent, but out of a consideration that neither the royal chamber nor the city of Orán had the right to set a fine in this instance, since neither of them had suffered any damages. It was a decision formulated strictly in agreement with the requirements of the law, and shows once again that Quiroga's decisions were based on strictly legal reasoning, even if they went against popular feeling.

But the lawsuit did not end there. A new mayor and resident magistrate, Dr. Sancho de Lebrija, arrived in the summer of 1526, and Quiroga had to give a report to him of his administration. On 11th August 1526, the lawyer Liminiana complained that his sentence against Caxines had been unjustly revoked by Quiroga, out of bad faith and merely to demonstrate that Caxines had done a bad job. In his defence petition, Quiroga showed a little anger, writing «the lawyer Quiroga, responding to this request or denunciation of that which has been expressed by the lawyer Liminiana, who says against me...». But in any case, Lebrija found in favour of Liminiana, and the case was submitted to the Royal Council. The final act of the lawsuit in Orán was carried out on 27th September 1526, when Quiroga pawned his possessions against a possible fine. That is the last date of any record with respect to Quiroga's activities in Orán.

When the trial was submitted to the Royal Council in October 1526, Quiroga wrote a letter defending his decision. This letter is one of the few documents that we possess which is entirely in his handwriting.

After the arrival of the new mayor, but before Quiroga returned to the Peninsula, he was called upon to carry out other official tasks. In accordance with a warrant issued in Granada on 23rd July 1526, while Quiroga was still in fact resident magistrate, he was commissioned to act as one of the representatives of the Crown of Castille in the signing of a new peace treaty with the King of Tremecén. The other Castilian representative was Pedro de Godoy, deputy to the field marshal of the Castilian forces in Ténez and Tremecén. Abdullah, the King of Tremecén, was represented by five ambassadors: two Moorish knights, the Sheikh of the Jews of Tremecén, and two Jewish servants of the King of Tremecén. It appears that there was a considerable dispute over the amount of tribute that the King of Tremecén should have to pay. He had offered an annual tribute of 5,000 Moorish doubloons. The Spanish wanted more, but Tremecén's representatives argued that their King could not give any more, as he had recently conquered the kingdom of his brother, the usurper Muley Mazote, and the country was bankrupt. Abdullah's ambassadors remained firm, to the point that they threatened to break off negotiations. The Castilians finally gave in on 2nd August 1526, and the new treaty was drafted and signed in the monastery of Santa Domingo el Real in Orán. It was later sent to Spain for royal approval, and was confirmed by King Carlos in Granada, on the 12th of the same month.

As the treaty was not exclusively Quiroga's work, it is hard to say to what extent he was responsible for its articles. The King of Tremecén was granted the right to send ambassadors to the King of Spain whenever he wished. The document established freedom of trade and migration between Tremecén and Orán, while enforced conversion of the subjects of the King of Tremecén to Christianity was prohibited. These articles show the sense of justice and fairness that has come to be associated with the name of Vasco de Quiroga.

On 25th October 1526, Quiroga returned to Granada, where King Carlos I was, with all his court. He must have also met there the future viceroy of Nueva España, Antonio de Mendoza, who was at court attending his elder brother Luis Hurtado de Mendoza, Count of Tendilla and field marshal of Granada.

Quiroga's work in Orán was, in many ways, a preparation for the type of work he would carry out on a larger scale in the New World. Orán was a recently conquered colony, and its conditions, which were still unstable, meant that relations between conquerors and conquered were not at all satisfactory. Quiroga's work there consisted of investigating the injustices of an official who had previously been sent by the Crown, but whose administration had led to complaints from different groups in the colony. He was also working in the region where most of the people did not possess a Hispanic culture and education. Quiroga would come up against the same problems in Nueva España, though with a wider scope and basic importance, and he would attempt to solve them with the same attention and care to the strict requirements of the law.

Map of the city of Algiers.
On the back is written: «a list of the captives and galleys and Turks that there are in
Algiers». M.P.D. VII-131

VASCO DE QUIROGA
AND THOMAS MORE'S *UTOPIA*

Ricardo León Alanís
Historical Research Institute
University of Michoacán

As we know, Vasco de Quiroga was sent to the New World in around 1530, to work as magistrate to the Second Audiencia of Mexico, and to remedy the serious damage that had been caused to Nueva España by the government headed by Nuño de Guzmán. In particularly, in the old indigenous domain of Michoacán, the actions of this renowned conquistador was seriously hampering the evangelical work that had only just been commenced, in around 1525, by several Franciscan missionaries; the damage was so great by then that the Tarascos (or Purepecha) – as the Indians of Michoacán were known – had fled to the mountains and were currently in a state of open rebellion.

And so, after discovering and investigating at first hand the sad situation of the lives of the indigenous people, subjected to slavery and very often exploited by the greed of some Spanish conquistadors, Vasco de Quiroga offered himself personally to remedy the terrible situation. And so, at the cost of his own salary and efforts, in around 1532 he founded the first Pueblo-Hospital of Santa Fe de los Altos, on the outskirts of Mexico City. Then in 1533, he opened the second Pueblo-Hospital of Santa Fe de la Laguna, on the banks of Lake Pátzcuaro, in the province of Michoacán.

In order to understand exactly the concept of these Pueblo-Hospitals de Santa Fe, we should bear in mind the fact that the Middle Ages in Spain, the term «hospital" was used in a much broader sense, to describe a charity-based institution set up to feed and educate the poor and defenceless, to look after the elderly and the sick, and to act as a place of shelter for pilgrims. This is why Vasco de Quiroga called the indigenous settlements that he created «Pueblo-Hospitals". In fact, it should be pointed out that in some accounts from that time, as well as other more recent works, these same congregations have been referred to as «Republics of Santa Fe".

Regulated and organised according to a series of Rules and Bylaws, which Vasco de Quiroga had created himself, the Pueblo-Hospitals were, at first, indigenous congregations made up of several families (both nuclear and extended) all descended from the same paternal lineage. In general terms, the indigenous nuclear family was considered to be comprised of six members (father, mother and an average of four children), even though apparently, these Pueblo-Hospitals began with a majority of extended families, comprising eight, 10 or even 12 married Indian couples with their respective children. However, when a family exceeded a certain number of members, a new family had to be formed. Each nuclear family was subject to the father's authority, who had to be respected and obeyed by all the members of the family. Fathers were responsible for marrying off their sons to the daughters of other families from the same Pueblo-Hospital or, alternatively, to the daughters of the poor people of the neighbourhood. Boys were considered to be marriageable at the age of 14, and girls at 12. In each extended family, all the members were obliged to obey the oldest grandfather; wives had to obey their husbands, and children had to serve and obey their parents, grandparents and great-grandparents. Thus there was no need to employ servants or maids from outside the immediate family. The Pueblo (settlement) as a whole was governed by an elected body chosen from all the fathers, made up of one Indian principal and three or four aldermen. The Indian principal had to be a good Christian and a man of an exemplary life; he should be humble and not too harsh, and should attempt to evoke love, honour and respect in everyone, though without becoming the object of scorn. His post would last for three years, though he could be re-elected for another term. The aldermen were selected annually, and this post was rotated between all the married men. In this governing body there were also another two fathers of families called jurists; these were Indians chosen by the principal and the aldermen, and they attended their meetings as representatives of the common interests of the people. These posts were rotated continually so that it was not always the same men representing the groups. The government meetings were carried out every third day in the house of the Indian principal. At these meetings, they discussed all the common issues of the Hospital-Pueblo, including the farms, boundaries and the work that had to be carried out collectively by all the inhabitants. No government agreement could be taken immediately, unless it was of great urgency; in general, each matter was discussed and analysed for two or three meetings before it went to the final vote.

In addition to the governing body made up of the Indians themselves, there was another authority: the priest-rector. This was a monk or secular cleric who was in charge of the religious administration of the Hospital-Pueblo. This man had to be informed of virtually everything that went on in the Hospital-Pueblo, while the more important agreements of the governing body also had to be approved by him. All complaints and disagreements by the Indians always had to be solved between them in an amicable manner, and in the presence of the rector, the Indian principal and the aldermen. Thus they avoided having to go to trial in the courts, to save money, as well as avoiding imprisonment and thus conserving the mutual coexistence and charity among all the inhabitants of the Hospital-Pueblo.

With respect to the subject of money and labour, the Hospital-Pueblos were organised in such a way that all the Indians worked for six hours every day for the benefit of the Hospital-Pueblo. Work was also considered to be as a means of learning and social coexistence, as a result of which it should be carried out willingly and without complaint. There were basically two types of work: craftwork and farm work. The main types of craftwork were, for the men, carpentry, building work, masonry and ironwork. Meanwhile, women were taught everything about fabric making, especially wool, linen, silk and cotton. The craftsmen trained in these skills were responsible for continuously repairing the communal buildings of the Hospital-Pueblo, as well as making the necessary tools for all the community, during their six hours of daily communal work.

However, agriculture was the main occupation, and virtually all the inhabitants of the Hospital-Pueblo worked on the land. The communal farms and ranches were worked by the members of all the families during their six hours of daily communal work, though sometimes it was more suitable for people to work from sunrise to sunset for two or three days in a row,

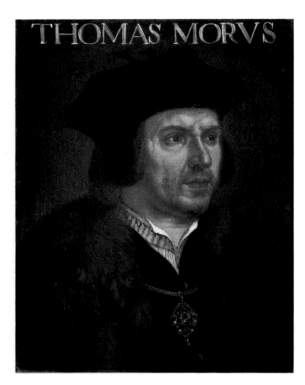

*Portrait of
Thomas More.
Giovianna Collection
Galleria degli Uffizi,
Florence.*

in accordance with timetables and weather changes of the season. During the fallow season, farm workers would carry out other supplementary work such as collecting wild food produce or cutting wood and working stone.

As well as growing cereal crops, farm workers also had to look after the chickens, turkeys, sheep, goats, cows, pigs and beasts of burden, mainly oxen. They also had to harvest the fruits and vegetables in the family orchards and gardens.

The resulting harvest of the communal work was distributed equally, in accordance with each family's needs, and no surplus would be handed out until the governors were sure that there would not be a food shortage the following year. To this end, in each Hospital-Pueblo there were specific places where agricultural produce was stored, and from where food was distributed to each family in accordance with their needs. In the event that there was a surplus of anything, it was especially used in a charitable sense, to benefit other people more needy than them. All the property of the Hospital-Pueblo was communally owned, even though each family could have their own small piece of land as a market garden, tilled for the purposes of recreation or to obtain a little subsidiary income. If profits were obtained through the sale of communal products, the money was kept in a chest that could only be opened using three keys – kept by the rector, the Indian principal and the oldest of the aldermen. This community chest was also used for storing account books, deeds and royal warrants referring to land and water sources, as well as other documents that were important for the Hospital-Pueblo.

With respect to the education and instruction of children, they had to learn from a very young age how to do agricultural work, at the same time as they were taught to read and write. And so, during school hours, they went twice a week to a field near the school where they would be taught about agriculture,

as if it were a game or pastime. As for the Indians' clothing, an attempt was made to maintain uniformity wherever possible, with simple, white garments that were made by the families themselves, without any decoration or costly embellishment. They were made of wool and cotton, and were suitable for use both in cold weather and in hot summers. They also had to be kept clean. The only significant difference consisted of the headdresses that the married women wore, to differentiate them from single young women.

It was compulsory for all the inhabitants of the Hospital-Pueblo to receive instruction in Christian and moral doctrine, as well as in good manners. To this end, Vasco de Quiroga ordered a catechism to be printed – or *Doctrina Cristiana* – that would teach the Indians not only about faith as good Christians, but also educate them in the general principles of civilised life. This catechism also marked the mass days and religious holidays that were to be held through the year at the Hospital-Pueblo. In general, this booklet was considered to be a complement to the Rules and Bylaws of the government, and was aimed at regulating everyday life in the community.

It is clear that Vasco de Quiroga's main aim in founding these Pueblo-Hospitals of Santa Fe was to provide the Indians that lived there with the basic principles of what was called «*mixta policía*» (mixed courtesy). This concept expressed the idea of good order and government (both temporal and spiritual) which would destroy only the worst of the Indians' pagan customs, while preserving all the good things of their previous way of life. And so, as Vasco de Quiroga said himself, the Indians were the «soft wax» or «blank slate» upon which he hoped to mould a new type of Christianity, similar to that of the Original Church – that is to say, like the Christianity of the early days of Jesus Christ and his apostles. In this way, the Indians educated at the Pueblo-Hospitals of Santa Fe would learn all the virtues that a good Christian should practice and at the same time would help to teach them to their fellow men and women.

Several studies (such as the ones by Sílvio Zavala and Joseph Benedict Warren) have shown that the Rules and Bylaws, as well as the communal organisation of the Pueblo-Hospitals of Santa Fe were undoubtedly inspired by *Utopia*, the famous work by Thomas More, which was first published in 1516. However, in order to adapt it to the New World, certain elements taken from the indigenous tradition were introduced, as well as others from the structure of Spanish municipal government. Furthermore, of course, the Christian rituals and customs were also incorporated. In fact, on this subject, Vasco de Quiroga declared in his *Information on Law* (written in 1535) that he had taken this plan" from the form of the republic" presented by the renowned English chancellor, whom he considered to be almost «inspired by the Holy Spirit», as he had succeeded in describing the state of the indigenous people and in presenting «a plan for a republic that was perfectly suited to the needs of natives», without having ever seen them. Thus, it can be said that one of the greatest ideals of European humanism – the dream of a utopian society, fairer and superior to the existing one – was fully attained in the Pueblo-Hospitals of Santa Fe, thanks to the work carried out by the magistrate of Mexico and first Bishop of Michoacán, Vasco de Quiroga.

A detail of the mural by the maestro Alfonso Villanueva
at the entrance to Uruapan.

VASCO DE QUIROGA

AND THE COLLEGE OF ST NICHOLAS IN PÁTZCUARO

Ricardo León Alanís
Historical Research Institute
University of Michoacán

The oldest reference to Vasco de Quiroga's plans to found a student's college in the bishopric of Michoacán dates back to 1538 when, in his capacity as Bishop elect, he took legal possession of the diocese in the old church that the Franciscan missionaries had built in the city of Tzintzuntzan. It is well known that, on the following day, Vasco de Quiroga moved to what was known as the «Pátzcuaro district" to take possession of the place and to build his church-cathedral there. At the same time, a significant event took place, as the Bishop elect also took possession of another site next to the previous one, where he would build «a college-hospital [sic] where the children of the natives and people of mixed race would be healed physically and educated and freed from the blindness and darkness of ignorance".

However, even though this declaration specifically stated that the college would be used for educating «the children of natives and people of mixed race", the organisation of the educational institution slowly began to adapt to the new circumstances, once Vasco de Quiroga had been definitively concentrated as Bishop and he began to fully organise the diocese of Michoacán. Thus, it is on record that in early 1540, when Quiroga returned from Mexico City, «he brought with him some priests and his chapel of students and choir, and later in Pátzcuaro, he began to build a house, and he said that it was for his students' college, because he did not want them to be in a place with a great many people, he preferred them to have more peace and quiet".

Unquestionably, the importance that the college founded by Vasco Quiroga in Pátzcuaro acquired must have been sufficiently great in those years, given that Bishop of Michoacán subsequently sent a report of it to the Spanish Crown. Shortly afterwards, on 1st May 1543, the Emperor Carlos I signed a warrant in Barcelona by which the college would be protected by loyal patronage. Incidentally, the warrant confusedly describes the foundation as «a college where the children of legitimate Spaniards and those of mixed race and some Indians who are linguists, and in order that they can make better use of same, will learn grammar and, in addition, the Indians will learn to speak our Castilian language, something which is very useful and necessary".

In this sense, another later warrant, dated in 1552, better defined the objectives of the college: «a college where Spanish schoolchildren will learn the language of the natives and the natives will learn the Castilian language, and everyone will be taught grammar and Christian doctrine". Or rather, the Spanish students that were brought up to serve as future priests in the diocese were in fact the only real students, though they would coexist with other Indian and mixed race pupils, with the aim that both would learn the Castilian and indigenous languages, as well as the Christian doctrine and Latin grammar.

During those years, Vasco de Quiroga achieved a number of royal favours to ensure the protection, support and economic maintenance of the college. Among these, there was the concession of a few plots of wasteland near Pátzcuaro, as well as other lands and farms − in the valley of Huaniqueo − which would be used for stock breeding, milling and fulling. However, during the early years in which Quiroga's project was in exist-ence, no mention was made of the fact that the college was to be dedicated to St. Nicholas, and until that time it was known only as the «College of Michoacán". In this respect, it is important to mention that the first accounts we have that refer to the «College of St. Nicholas" must have been connected with the journey and temporary stay of Vasco de Quiroga in Spain (1547-1554), as in fact it was only shortly before his return to Michoacán that the church began to be commonly referred to under this name. In this respect, there are two more very good reasons for why Vasco de Quiroga wanted his college at Michoacán to be given the sacred dedication of St. Nicholas the Bishop. First, because this Saint was the patron saint of the town of Madrigal (Spain), the first Bishop of Michoacán's place of birth, and secondly (and more importantly) that ever since medi-aeval times, St. Nicholas the Bishop had been considered the patron saint and protector of students. And so, we can be sure that when he chose St. Nicholas the Bishop as the patron of his college, Vasco Quiroga wanted the saint to become the spiritual protector of the student congregation.

And so, on 24th January 1565, the first Bishop of Michoacán submit-ted to his papal secretary a «report and declaration" which has generally been considered as his testament. In this document, for the first time, Vasco de Quiroga takes great care in listing a series of regulations for the college; thus, Vasco de Quiroga's testament can therefore be considered to be the legal and official constitutive charter of the College of St. Nicholas the Bishop and the Pueblo-Hospitals of Santa Fe as being holy works. However, while the college and the hospitals had already existed for several years at this point, and had even been under the protection of royal patronage since 1543, they had still lacked the juridical basis that would give them greater legal support, and fact this basis was definitively established from the moment when Vasco de Quiroga announced his testament, and instituted the College of St. Nicholas the Bishop and the Pueblo-Hospitals of Santa Fe as holy works. He also gave them their first Rules and Bylaws, or formal constitutions and statutes.

Proof of this is the fact that repeated mention is made in his testament to the College of St. Nicholas (using this specific dedicatory name), and that all its general objectives and characteristics are clearly defined − something that was lacking in all the previous documents. And so, with respect to the original aims with which the college was created, Bishop Quiroga pointed out, clearly and for the first time, that the objective of the foundation was to «remedy the great lack of ministers of holy sacrament and divine worship that has existed in our bishopric of Michoacán, and still exists, and that they should be presbyters and linguists". To this end, Bishop Quiroga ordered that at the College of St. Nicholas, «we should take in and bring up *pure Spanish* students who are more than 20 years old and who want to be ordained and are linguists, and thus, or-dained from all the orders, they will help to remedy the aforementioned great lack of ministers".

In other words, the Bishop of Michoacán meant that, in order to be able to enrol in the college and be ordained as presbyters and ministers

EDUCATION IN THE DAYS OF VASCO DE QUIROGA

Igor Cerda Farías
Ex-monastery of Tiripetío
University of Michoacán

The world of education in the 16th century was very different to the one we know today, right from the lowest levels to what we would today consider to be university level; this is because subjects and syllabi were strongly framed and determined by the Christian religion. There was no direct continuity in education from a basic level to a higher one, so that one could not expect that someone who had completed his basic education could immediately carry on studying at a middle school. Among the deciding factors were the lack of schools, the type of instruction offered there, the institutions that were capable of running schools, the ethnic group at which education was aimed and the cost of schooling within the society that they lived in. Thus, one cannot speak of a single way of teaching, but of specific projects created by the religious orders of the Augustines and the Franciscans, especially by the Bishop Vasco de Quiroga.

In the year 1540, a little over two years after Vasco de Quiroga took possession of his bishopric in the city of Pátzcuaro, he embarked on the task of creating a college in which sons of Spaniards over 20 years of age would be educated in the space of four years, during which time they would study morals, Latin and the language of the indigenous peoples with the basic aim of becoming ordained as presbyters. The college, called St. Nicholas the Bishop, was granted royal patronage by the Emperor Carlos I in 1545. This project took place in parallel with another of Quiroga's great social projects, the Pueblo-Hospital of Santa Fe de la Laguna which, more than a simple educational centre, represented the achievement of an ideal — a place which would lay the foundations for Quiroga's project of creating an indigenous society where communal benefits and life in an ordained congregation, organised under the rectorship of the church, would result in the creation of new Christians. And this project, naturally, could not be separated from education, which was conceived as an everyday exercise in the instruction and training of all the members of the hospital, no matter their age or sex. The teaching stipulated in the Rules and Bylaws created by Quiroga was organised under the form of gender, as while the boys were instructed in agriculture and family skills, the girls were educated in domestic work, specifically the manufacture of fabrics, embroidery, sewing, cooking and tilling the family market garden, not forgetting their role as moral guardians within the family.

The efforts made by Vasco de Quiroga's diocesan clergy to educate the children was not the only work they did in Michoacán, as the clerics from the orders of St. Francis and St. Augustine also carried out ambitious educational projects related with the indigenous society project through the founding of monastery schools. While the common denominator in these schools was the teaching of Christian doctrine and the basic principles of education — learning to read, write, count and sing — significant differences existed with respect to who the education was aimed at, and the type of knowledge that was taught there.

The Franciscans, who were immersed in millennialist ideals and original Christianity, viewed Indians as minor, as people with little sense, and whose lives should be seen as a journey through the world for the purpose of achieving eternal life; as a result, they should be guided and protected along the path to salvation. Ever since their arrival in Michoacán in 1525, their educational efforts had been based on the children, who would be the only ones among the inhabitants of the indigenous towns who would be taught to read and write by the monks. The idea was to gradually mould them so that they would become transmitters to the rest of the population of the new faith and the new values coming from Spain. The teaching that was carried out inside the monastery college, to the children of the principals and to some of the children that showed greater aptitude, was not given with the intention of making the children erudite in the subjects they were studying, rather it was a question of training people so they could reproduce the social order that the church aimed to establish, called «Christian courtesy". By excluding most of the population from a more formal education, the continuity of the governing organisations was reaffirmed, given that these children would be the ones who would carry out the role of governing and administrating within their communities in the future.

The monastery schools of the monks of St. Francis did not consider teaching adults or people from the plains, as these people showed a natural inclination for learning diverse manual skills, such as pottery, basket-making, agriculture, sewing, trade or any other skill of indigenous origin or from Spain.

Meanwhile, the monks from the order of St. Augustine, who had arrived in Michoacán in the year 1537, established a large-scale educational program in which not only the children or clergy could receive some type of instruction, but anybody who was interested. The focal point of this project, in accordance with the order's very positive view of the indigenous peoples, was the town of Tiripetío, where three types of education coexisted simultaneously:

1) The education typical of a monastery school, where children were educated in a way that was more or less similar to the education given in Franciscan monasteries, even though in this town, all the children could learn to read and write, and not only the children of noblemen or principals. This was a change that was not only qualitative but also quantitative, in that it offered knowledge to areas of the population that did not necessarily form part of the indigenous government.

2) During the early years of novo hispana existence in this town, the encomendero Juan de Alvarado succeeded in bringing all the way from Mexico a group of Spanish craftsmen and teachers of different trades, who taught their skills to the Indians. In a short time, the Indians succeeded in becoming teachers of other Indians, to create what was perhaps the largest craft centre in the bishopric of Michoacán. In Tiripetío, one could find locksmiths, cobblers, tailors, painters, gilders, sculptures, masons, scribes, blacksmiths, carpenters, musicians, lathe operators, dyers, feather workers, silversmiths, and many others. In fact, there was so much specialisation among the Indians of Tiripetío that many of them left the town to go off and teach their skills to other Indian towns; however, this partly led to their ruin, because, as the Augustine chronicler Brother Mathías de Escobar wrote, «those who left, did not return...»

3) The third type of education that existed in this town had a universal nature, as it was where, in the early months of 1541, the first higher education studies were offered on the American continent. Under the direction of Brother Alonso de la Vera Cruz, a course in Arts and Theology began in the monastery of Tiripetío; the contents of the course were similar to those taught in universities in Europe. The teaching of the arts consisted of learning the seven free disciplines of the Trivium (grammar, logic, dialectics and rhetoric) and the Cuadrivium (geometry, arithmetic, astronomy and music). Studies in theology comprised the study of the Holy Scriptures, the thoughts of St. Augustine, St. Thomas Aquinas, St. Albert Magnus, St. Buenaventura and many other great thinkers of the early and late Middle Ages. To encourage the students more, the teacher Vera Cruz installed a library in the monastery — the first to exist in America. Arts studies were not only considered basic for a monk's education, they formed part of the education that anyone could receive. Because when these courses were opened in Tiripetío, entrance was not restricted to anybody, and they were attended by the monks, diocesan clerics based in Pátzcuaro, young Spaniards who were the sons of farmers and encomenderos, as well as some indigenous people who belonged to the ancient noble line of Michoacán, one of the most outstanding of whom was Antonio Huitziméngari, the son of the last king of Michoacán, who made great strides in his education, learning Latin, a great deal of Greek and the basics of Hebrew.

The basic aim of creating this educational centre in Tiripetío was to train the monks and novices in the field of theology, linguistics (the study of indigenous languages) and other disciplines that would be useful to them in effectively carrying out the ultimate aim of their presence in the New World: the evangelisation of the natives. Establishing these courses was of great importance to the Augustines, as they laid the foundations — legal, theological and administrative — for dealing with the problems that came up day by day as a consequence of the consolidation and expansion of Nueva España; these problems included the ability of the Indians to receive the sacrament, the payment of tithes, the rights of the Indians, the legality of the payment of tributes, colonial farming and even the Spanish conquest.

Finally, we must not forget that while the regular and secular clergy were developing their educational program, the Guayangareo chapter had also embarked on the task of setting up an educational centre for Spaniards living in the region. Taking as its focus the Franciscan teaching that had existed before 1541, the College of St. Michael based its curricula on three areas: learning to read, write and count, just as students learned in any school on the Iberian Peninsula. The founding of the College of St. Michael of Guayangareo, unlike the aforementioned schools, was carried out in response to a need to reproduce the culture of the parents and grandparents as a hegemonic group in the children of their Spanish neighbours. As a result, the civil chapter responded to the population's demands that their children be taught doctrine and education by taking over the patronage of the college with respect to its financial administration, regulation and supervision of the private tutors and teachers necessary for training the pupils. This educational centre — which was the first municipal school in all of Nueva España —survived until 1580, when it was merged with the College of St. Nicholas the Bishop, which had recently been moved to what was then the city of Valladolid.

The time of Vasco de Quiroga, practically in the second and third quarter of the 16th century — was a time of great advances with respect to education in Michoacán, and the impact of this left a lasting mark on the nascent Michoacán society for many years after the Bishop's death. Even though it must be said that the educational projects were not similar in any way, they all sought to give the best education to the youth of Nueva España, influenced by the clear and differentiated social projects of the different institutions that promoted them.

VASCO DE QUIROGA IN TZINTZUNTZAN
FROM YRECHEQUARO TARASCO
TO THE INDIAN AND SPANISH CITY OF MICHOACÁN

J. Ricardo Aguilar González

Historical Research Institute

University of Michoacán

On the southern shore of Lake Pátzcuaro there are traces of what was once the most important pre-Hispanic capital in western Mexico. The most prominent buildings of this urban complex are the various platforms and terraces, as well as five *yácatas* (the pre-Hispanic Tarasco monumental buildings with a characteristic «keyhole» shape). These structures enabled their owners to rule a large part of the lake. On the arrival of the Spanish, the city was the centre of military, religious, economic and political activity in the pre-Hispanic Tarasco state. The Tarasco Indians called the city Tzintzuntzan («The place of hummingbirds»), while the Mexicans, and later the Spaniards, called it Huitzitzilan. During the 16th century it was better known as the «city of Mechuacan», in reference to the existence of the rich lakes in the Tarasco landscape. It was also where the supreme governor (the *Irecha* or *Cazonci*) lived, as well as most of his functionaries and relatives. There were also the people called the «Purepecha», who were skilled at working with precious metals, textiles and pottery. At its height, Tzintzuntzan was a dynamic centre where tributes arrived and were redistributed; these tributes included animal skins, firewood, *pulque*, corn, pumpkins, beans, chilli, ceramics, black and grey obsidian, different types of cotton blankets, various fruits, salt, fish, copper, gold, silver and imported goods from other latitudes such as turquoise, green obsidian and different species of poultry.

Vasco de Quiroga participated in two of the events in the city's colonial history, which in turn marked two periods in his own life. In the first of these he was a lawyer, a judge in the Second *Audiencia*, and his main concern was dispensing justice to the Indians who had suffered humiliation and bad treatment at the hands of the Spanish authorities in Michoacán, as well as teaching them the «Christian» way of life. By the second of these events, Quiroga had been invested as Bishop elect of the recently founded bishopric of Michoacán, and he promptly moved Tzintzuntzan's pre-eminence to Pátzcuaro, a place where he believed he could find the ideal conditions for his model of coexistence between Indians of different populations and Spaniards, all of them linked by a monumental church-cathedral. As a judge he did succeed, it is true, in laying the foundations for creating social links (known as «living in courtesy», in order and justice) between the Tarasco indigenous people.

The history of the Uacúsecha

The history of the ancient settlers of Michoacán was compiled and written between 1538 and 1541 by the Franciscan Brother Jerónimo de Alcalá. He recorded the testimony of Indians who experienced the process of Spanish occupation and organisation, as well as helping the painters - *caracha* – who illustrated the text known as the *Account of Michoacán*. The tale is about how a collection of related groups that controlled different populations in the Michoacán basins got involved in a dispute over territory and their respective supremacy. Each group was backed by

one of the five *tirípemencha* gods, which accompany them in battle and appear to them in their dreams to give them advice. Of these, the god *Curicaueri* was the guardian god of the group of eagles – or *uacúsecha* – which was the group that succeeded at that time – through a series of political alliances, war, negotiation and marriage with the natives of the islands – in controlling all the area around Lake Pátzcuaro.

The *uacúsecha* were great hunters, and were skilled in the use of the bow and arrow, in tanning hides, and in cooking their prey. *Curicaueri* was a bellicose god who demanded that they feed him constantly with huge bonfires that were never allowed to go out, as well as with the blood of the *uacúsecha* themselves, «Hiripan and Tangaxoan sacrificed their ears, and everyone, because of having been able to defeat them», as well as the ones that were captured in battle. A governor needed a «piece» of this god – a lump of black obsidian – if he wanted to lead his people to war. *Curicaueri* was able to make his enemies ill and to win battles, and this is why every warlike exploit was offered up to him.

The *Account of Michoacán* includes the story of the Tarasco hero-governor Taríacuri (*circa* 1300-1350) who, based in a «district of Pázcuaro called Tarímichúndiro» led the strategy of the control, negotiation, consolidation and expansion of the Uacúsecha, within and beyond the region of Pátzcuaro. Taríacuri's wanderings around the region help him to win support from other governments, such as those of Cumachuén, Erongarícuaro, Hurichu and Pichátaro, at the same time as he settles his quarrels with others, such as the towns of Curínguaro and Taríaran. In his old age, Taríacuri calls his three disciples to a «little mountain called Thiapu» in Pátzcuaro where he had built three piles of earth, which resemble three hills, «and placed on top of each one a stone and an arrow». The «boys» arrive at the place, but they cannot find Taríacuri, they only see the three heaps with a symbol of the control of the land on top – an arrow. Taríacuri then appears and said to them:

Hear me, my sons: look, Hirepan, here we have three lords. You are on this pile, the one in the middle, which is the town of Cuyacan [Ihuatzio], and you, Tangaxoan, are on this pile, which is the town of Michuacan [Tzintzuntzan], and you, Hiquíngaje, are on this one, which is the town of Pazcuaro. Thus we have our three lords.

And so, in around 1350, the city of Tzintzuntzan was founded, sharing its importance with Ihuatzio, «the house of the coyote» and Pátzcuaro, an old settlement of the ancestors of Taríacuri where the foundations can still be found of abandoned temples that were reused by the Uacúsecha dwellers. Once the governments of the basin had been shared out strategically between his nephews Hiripan, Tangaxoan and his youngest son Hiquíngaje, all of them *quangariecha* («brave men»), a series of conquests began, in which first Taríaran was defeated, and afterwards Curínguaro, after which they expanded beyond the basin of Pátzcuaro Lake. The battles and attacks began to spread toward the east, thereby conquering Tiripetío, Etúcuaro and Tetepeo, and from there, northeast via Huaniqueo, Chucándiro and Teremendo; after that, the conquerors travelled

Fragment of Juan O'Gorman's mural History of Michoacán, Gertrudis Bocanegra Library, Patzcuaro.

along the sierra to the west of Lake Pátzcuaro (known at that time as the Tarasca Sierra), to conquer Comachuén, Naranjan, Zacapu, Cherán, Savinan and Uruapan, after which they travelled southwest to reach Urecho. At each town they conquered, they collected the «treasure» of the defeated governor, and which was comprised of «jewels... and gold and silver» as well as feathers: «green and white plumes, and coloured plumage». All of this booty was sent to Ihuatzio, where it was kept. Part of this «treasure» was the gods of the different towns that they conquered, and which they added to the worship of the state religion. These warriors were responsible for bringing together, once again, all the «highly bred» gods; that is, the *Tiripemencha* brothers of *Curicaueri*, which led to the planning of the temple of Tzintzuntzan, as we shall see later on.

Expansion continued through other *quangariecha* from the island of Jarácuaro and through those who had supported the enterprise of Taríacuri and his disciples. Tangaxoan, Hiquíngaje and Hiripan became the leaders of the campaigns and governed from the three main cities, particularly from Ihuatzio, as it was the residence of the god *Curicaueri*. Thus,

the subsequent conquests were carried out to safeguard the towns that lay on the tributaries of the river Balsas, in Tierra Caliente to the south-south-west, Cuitzeo Lake and the region to the northeast, the northern strip of the river Lerma and the Chapala-Sayula basin to the east.

THE YRECHEQUARO, "PLACE OF THE KINGDOM"

At the end of the work carried out by Taríacuri, his son and his nephews, a new generation took control of the Tarasco state. Hiripan, Lord of Ihuatzio, had a son called Ticátame, who duly passed on power on to Zizíspandaquare, son of Tangaxoan, Lord of Tzintzuntzan. As the *Account of Michoacán* describes it:

In the time of Ticáteme, Lord of Cuyacan [Ihuatzio], the main city became Michuacan [Tzintzuntzan] which led Zizízpandaquare to base *Curicaueri* in Michuacan [Tzintzuntzan] together with all the treasure. He stored some of it in the lake, on some islands, and some in his house".

Zizispandáquare was the first governor to base *Curicaueri* in Tzintzuntzan together with «all the treasure"; he did so in 1454, and it meant that henceforth all power was concentrated on his person. From that point on, the leading Tarasco governor began to be known as *Irecha*, meaning «he who dwelt there and possessed the entire world". Thus, in 1580, the Tiripetío councillor Pedro Montes de Oca tells us that:

This name *Irecha* is like saying «King", even though each king had his particular name, because one was called Tzintzincha *Irecha*, and another Zuangua *Irecha*, which is like saying Carlos King, Felipe King.

However, colonial sources referred to this dignitary as *Cazonci*, owing to the fact that in the centre of Mexico he was known as the «lord of the countless houses". Zizipandáquare was forced to resist (with the aid of the Otomís and the Matlazincas) the military incursions of the Mexicans who, at this time (1476-1477) were ruled by Axayácatl. This rivalry continued for the next two decades. Under Ahuízotl's rule, Mexican incursions focused on seeking control of the river Balsas, while both groups (the Tarascos and the Mexicans) carried out defence and attack strategies in Taximaroa, Ostuma, Acámbaro and Cutzamala. In 1517-1518, a Mexican offensive took place, led by the Tlaxcalteca warrior Tlahuicole, under the rule of Moctezuma II. Zizizpandáquare responded by consolidating his borders. The *Account of Sirándaro and Gayameo*, written by the councillor and first mayor of mines Hernando de Coria in 1579, relates that all the tributes from the towns of Cusio, Sirándaro and Guayameo (which were in the area along the river Balsas) were taken to the border town of Cutzamala to feed the Tarasco soldiers, as well as the *Purépecha* (this word also refers to the people who were taken to the battles by force) who comprised the conscription.

The tributes they gave to the King of Mechoacan [Tzintzuntzan], included taking him things and possessions and sowing corn, which by way of tribute they took to the town of Cutzamala, which lies six leagues from this town, and there it was distributed and consumed because the King of Mechoacan [Tzintzuntzan] had in that town of Cutzamala more than 10,000 soldiers, who were fighting the war against those from Mexico and guarding the border, and they travelled as far as the province of Ostuma, which belonged to Montezuma.

The consequences of this conflict continued until the arrival of the Spanish, thereby preventing cooperation between Mexicans and Tarascos in their resistance of the invaders. After Zizizpandácuare, the next *Irecha* was his son Zuangua, who came to power in 1479 and ruled until 1520. During these latter two reigns, the city of Tzintzuntzan became the receiver of tributes from all the territory under Tarasco rule. It was also the headquarters of most of the Army (some 10,000 men in the basin alone), as well as of the bureaucracy and the craftsmen specialised in making religious and political paraphernalia. It was also the seat of the high priests, the central point from which the four cardinal points were measured (the «four parts" of the world) and the place where *Curicaueri* was looked after. The god had been brought here together with his four *Tiripemencha* god brothers, to whom the five *yácatas* were built. These structures were a symbol of the union between all the «highly bred" Gods — all those gods

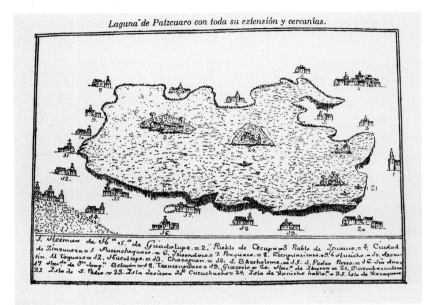

Lake Pátzcuaro, showing all of the lake and the surrounding area.

who, because of their origins, closely rooted in the Tarasco identity, and because of their warlike skills, stood above any other god that might form part of the Tarasco pantheon. Moreover, Tzintzuntzan became the *Yrechequaro* — «the place of the kingdom" and the dwelling of the *Irecha*, who had been chosen to govern by *Curicaueri*. The 18th century Franciscan chronicler Pablo de la Purísima Concepción Beaumont expresses it thus:

What is beyond doubt is that Muchoacán had many kings with absolute power, and that Tzintzuntzan was always the seat of their government, to the extent that even today one can see the ruins of the royal palace close by this ancient city, previously the town of Yguatzio, and the beautiful square has been conserved, though its carved stone walls are almost ruined; and on the banks of Lake Siragüen there are ancient monuments of things that were for the enjoyment of kings and lords, while other ruined buildings that can be found in other places.

However, the pre-Hispanic city of Tzintzuntzan was to undergo dramatic transformations after the Spaniards approached the Tarasco-Mexican border, and even more so when the first Spanish institutions became established in the province of Michoacán.

THE SPANISH ARRIVE AT TZINTZUNTZAN OR HUITZITZILAN

The arrival of the Spanish in Michoacán had been predicted by a series of omens and dreams. Two comets were sighted, people dreamt of animals that had never been seen before, and some buildings began to shed the slabs that decorated them. All these signs and premonitions came from all over Tarasco territory, and were reported to Zuangua *Irecha* in the capital of Tzintzuntzan. However, the omen experienced by

Fragments of Juan O'Gorman's mural History of Michoacán,
Gertrudis Bocanegra Library, Patzcuaro.

offerings, because as from now things will not be so. You must not play your drums anymore: break them all. There must be no more temples or bonfires, and no more smoke must be raised. Everything must be stripped because now other men will come to these lands, and they will travel to the ends of the earth, with a right hand and the left hand, and as far as the shores of the sea, and they will move ahead and there will be but one poem, and there will not be many poems as we have had, only one single one throughout the regions of the earth.

And so from that point on, there would be one single poem, and the poem would be «all one»: this was a way of explaining that the «Council of gods" would have to ends to give way to the one god, the one who would rule «all the areas of the earth". And so, the arrival of the Spanish in Michoacán caused a dramatic change in the policy of the *Irecechequa*. Even before any Europeans reached the capital, smallpox had been brought by one of the messengers sent by Cuitláhuac or Cuauhtémoc before the siege of Mexico-Tenochtitlan. One victim of this illness was Zuangua *Irecha*, who died in 1520 and was survived by nine sons and several daughters. Out of these, the few advisers, the «old men" or *Curaecha* who advised the *Cazonci* and the lords who governed the *Camahchacuhpecha* towns that survived the disease jointly chose Zuangua's first-born son, Tangaxoan Zizincha.

The new *Irecha* was surrounded by murky characters such as Timas (who, before the imminent arrival of Cristóbal of Olid to Tzintzuntzan, advised the new leader to drown himself in the lake) as well as ambiguous, obliging types such as Cuiniarángari (who was later baptised Pedro), who was the main guide for the Spanish throughout the *Irecechequa*, as well as being the first to mention the existence of the *Cazonci*'s «treasure".

Cristóbal de Olid entered Tzintzuntzan on 25th July 1522 accompanied by thousands of Mexican allies. During his stay, he acted as governor and dispenser of justice, even though he soon revealed that his main objective was to find the «treasure" which, as I have mentioned, the predecessors of Tangaxoan Zinzincha had accumulated over the past 150 years, and which was stored on the islands of Janitzio, Pacandan, Apúpato and Urandén as well as in the capital Tzintzuntzan. Cristóbal de Olid was the first of many Spanish governors who came here bent on seeking treasure, and who had little concern for government or justice in the province of Michoacán and its capital city.

Hernán Cortés, who acknowledged Tzintzuntzan as a city and tried to found a Spanish town with the same men that De Olid had brought, had a meeting with Tangaxoan Zizincha in the city of Mexico or «Temixtitan" [Tenochtitlan], and made him sign an agreement by which the *Cazonci* or *Irecha* promised to hand over the tributes from the Indians that arrived in the capital every 20 days to the Spaniards which Captain Cortés would appoint for the administration of the land. Thus, in 1523 and 1524, Antonio de Caravajal travelled through the Tarasco *Irecechequa* together with several Indians and interpreters. He explained how much each town would have to pay and where they would have to take the tributes, at the same time as he acted as head of justice and govern-

the daughter of a «principal" (or *camahchacuhpeti*) from Ucareo revealed that one age was coming to an end, and a new one was beginning. An eagle had appeared to her and led her to a mountain called Xanoata Hucazio. There she found all the gods in «a very big house", the gods «of the left-hand and the right hand": *Xaratanga*, the goddess of Jarácuaro, the five «highly bred" *Tiripemencha* gods (*Curicaueri*'s brothers) and *Curita Caheri*, the «messenger of the gods". Of these, *Tiripeme quarencha* warned them of the coming of new men and the end of the old gods, and he ordered them to give up any attempt at being worshipped.

Go to your homes all of you, do not take with you that wine that you carry; break all those jugs, which you will no longer have in the future as you have had until now, when we were very prosperous. Smash up the wine vessels, stop your human sacrifices and do not bring any more

ment. Cortés was put in charge of several mines, as well as the city of Tzintzuntzan, to which he referred using the *Náhuatl* name Huitzitzilan or «Uchichila", and its «districts". Following the agreement between the *Cazonci* or *Irecha* and Cortés, the Tarasco *Irecechequa* was reorganised, and henceforth it was referred to as the «province of Michoacán".

One year after Tangaxoan's visit to Cortés, the Franciscan fathers arrived, on a mission to bring to an end the natives' idolatrous practices and to impose Christianity. Brother Martín de Jesús (or de la Coruña), with the consent of Tangaxoan Zinzincha (who by that time had been baptised Francisco in the city of Mexico), arrived in Tzintzuntzan to begin building Michoacán's first church. Francisco Tangaxoan Zizincha gave them a site next to his dwelling, on a platform on Yaguarato mountain, north of the *yácatas*. The small church was dedicated to St. Anne, and was consecrated in 1526. However, the chapel did not stay long on the site, as it was soon moved to where the ex-monastery and church of St. Francis can be found today in Tzintzuntzan.

From 1524 to 1528, relations were hostile between the *encomenderos* of the province with the Indians. The Indians suffered abuse in the work

they were ordered to do, as a result of which they rebelled and disobeyed the orders they received to move from their homes to go and work in the mines. As a result, the graduate Juan de Ortega was sent to the province with orders to dispense justice, impose government and order the towns to start paying their tributes again.

Nevertheless, the situation worsened with the first *Audiencia* that was headed by Nuño Beltrán de Guzmán between 1529 and 1531. His governorship was a particularly terrible one for the Tarasco Indians – in the early days of 1530, he arrested Francisco Tangaxoan Zizincha and took him to the river Lerma in Puruándiro. There, he was subjected to a summary trial, and accused of having received tributes from the towns and of having set up an ambush against the Spanish. Thus on 14th February he was executed, his body incinerated and his ashes scattered on the river. After his death, Pedro Cuiniérengari took over the post of governor of the Indians in the city and province of Michoacán.

Meanwhile, the Spanish authorities in charge of justice and government were more concerned over the administration of the mines in the south of the province. This was the case with the first mayor Alonso de

Tabernacle church in Pátzcuaro.

Vasco de Quiroga figures as one of the great founders in the consciousness of the Mexican state.

Doctor Silvio Zavala

The Vasco de Quiroga Route runs through privileged
locations in the biodiversity of Michoacán;
the scenes of one of the most
important humanistic projects
in the history of America.

On the way to the P'urhépecha Meseta.

Following pages:
Lake Pátzcuaro.

P'urhépecha Meseta.

Lake Pátzcuaro.

In the Canyon of the
Eleven Peoples.

Wild flowers in Michoacán.

Palms on the banks of the
river Cupatitzio.

Maguey and butterfly
on the shore of Lake
Pátzcuaro.

Waterfall at Chorros
del Varal.

Archaeological site of
Las Yacatas, the remains
of the pre-Hispanic
ceremonial centre.

Vasco de Quiroga first arrived at Tzintzuntzan, "the place of the hummingbirds", capital of the P'urhépecha empire, and where he was invested as the first Bishop of Michoacán.

Hundred-year-old olive trees in the atrium of
the monastery at Tzintzuntzan; tradition has
it that they were planted by Vasco de Quiroga.

🌿 *The fame of this celebrated gentlemen spread far and wide to distant
regions, and this is how he became known to many indians who no army
had succeeded in dominating, subjecting or defeating; and just because of
the fame of this holy Bishop, they spontaneously and freely came to him,
producing great shows of rejoicing.*

*Portrait of the first Bishop of Michoacán
Cristóbal Cabrera, 16th century.*

Following pages:
A space in the monastery of Tzintzuntzan that has been
restored by the organisation Adopt a Work of Art.

🌿 *If it should be necessary to build or repair the church, or to
construct another, or to rebuild it, all of you should work on it
together, and you should help each other with great determination,
encouraging each other.*

Vasco de Quiroga's Rules and Bylaws.

Previous pages:
Work on building the Franciscan monastery
at Tzintzuntzan began in the 16th century.

Frescoes in Tzintzuntzan monastery.

Daybreak at Lake
Pátzcuaro.

The lake region of
Pátzcuaro was one of
the main settings for
Quiroga's work. Visitors
can take the scenic route
or go on the boat trip
to the islands..

Janitzio seen from the
island of Yunuén.

The town of San Jerónimo
Purenchécuaro seen from
the restaurant and chalets
at Cerro del Sandio.

The island of Janitzio.

Fishermen from the island of Janitzio showing
how they use their butterfly nets.

Fisherman from Janitzio
with his butterfly net.

Stork on the island
of Yunuen.

A road on the P'urhépecha meseta.

All of you must know how to work well and to be occupied and skilled in the work of agriculture from childhood, with great willingness and determination. When they go to work in the fields, all of those from a family should go together, with the wife's father. This will be a great example to encourage others.

Rules and bylaws
of Don Vasco

Craftsman weaving
plant fibres.

Market at Zacán.

P'urhépecha woman from Patamban.

Members of a cooperative from Apatzingan.

The conquistadors soon realized that Vasco de Quiroga was not going to favour them, and so they went off to found Valladolid; 29 families remained in Pátzcuaro, who inter-mixed with the hard-working purépecha people. Our fathers and teachers taught us from a very young age, love, respect and generation for Vasco de Quiroga; we learned where Madrigal de las Altas Torres was before we did the location of New York, until it seemed as if I had been there myself. That is how we feel; if someone comes from there, we like to give him food and hospitality, we push the boat out.

Enrique Soto Gonzalez
Chronicler of Pátzcuaro

Plaza Vasco de Quiroga, Pátzcuaro.

Pátzcuaro was chosen by Vasco de Quiroga as the location for his bishopric and work. His projects are still present in the form of the town's layout, the founding of the College of St. Nicholas and his plans to build his great basilica, where his physical remains lie.

central figures of which
was Vasco de Quiroga.

Calle Madrigal de las Altas
Torres in Pátzcuaro.

A corridor in the Hotel
Hacienda Mariposas
in Pátzcuaro.

Following pages:
The woodland by the
Pátzcuaro Hotel Hacienda
Mariposas.

Morelia Cathedral.

Courtyard of the old College of
St. Nicholas in Pátzcuaro.

Statue of Vasco de Quiroga in the Garden of Roses, Morelia.

*The movements that have shaken Mexico, since its independence to the
great struggle for democracy, have all come from Michoacán, from the
seed sown by Vasco de Quiroga at the College of St. Nicholas.*

Enrique Soto González
Chronicler of Pátzcuaro

Following pages:
College of St. Nicholas in Morelia, Michoacán.

Pueblo-Hospital of Zacán.

One of the most attractive features of the Vasco de Quiroga Route is the network
of chapels with magnificent coffering, and which have been restored by the civil
association Adopt a Work of Art. In addition to their invaluable artistic value,
they are testimonies to the first encounters between Spaniards — still very
much under the influence of Islam — and the indigenous artistry that
generated one of the first expressions of mixed-race Mexico.

Chapel of Santa Rosa
de Lima in Zacán.

Following pages:
Coffering in the chapel of
Santa Rosa de Lima, Zacán.

A view of the atrium in
the church of Tupataro.

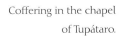

Coffering in the chapel
of Tupátaro.

Following pages:
Detail of the coffering in
the chapel of Tupátaro.

Detail of the coffering in
the chapel of Tupátaro.

The church of Santiago Nurio.

Following pages:
Decorated ceiling of the choir at
the church of Santiago Nurio.

Chapel of the Pueblo-
Hospital of Nurio.

REGINA
PATRIAR
CARUM

Detail of the coffering in the chapel of the Pueblo-Hospital of Nurio.

Detail of the façade of the church of Angahuan.

Loggia at the
Conservatory de las Rosas.

Altarpiece at the church
of Santa Rosa de Lima
in Morelia.

A cluster of monarch butterflies at the Monarch Reserve, Michoacán.

The hands of a craftsman
lacquering a piece
in Pátzcuaro.

About to begin a dance
at the Festival of
P'urhépecha Culture.

Young people from Zacán
welcoming travellers
on the Quetzal Route.

❧ You will set aside some days for your main holidays when you will eat all together, and make merry. The costs of such celebrations should be paid for by everyone, according to the abundance of the dishes, and all very cheerful with careful decoration.

Rules and Bylaws de Don Vasco.

Details of P'urhépecha women's clothing.

Dance of the old people.

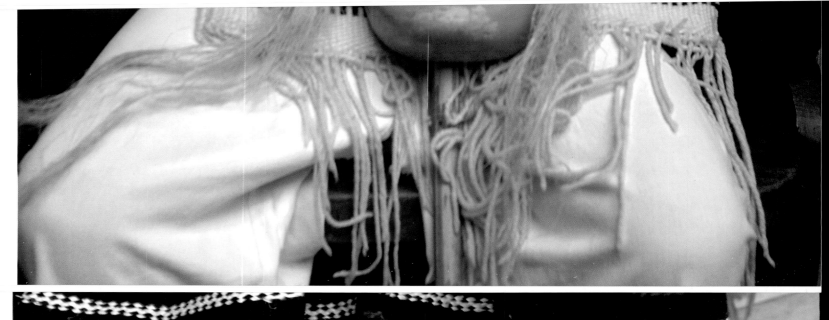

Pine cones from Patamban

Ceramic pieces at the craft
market in Tzintzuntzan.

Mask from Pátzcuaro.

Wooden pieces in
Pátzcuaro market.

Carving a column
in Tzintzuntzan.

Shawls from Ahuiran.

Following pages:
Shawl with feathers.

Orchids.

The source of the river Cupatitzio, the "singing river", in the national park within the city of Uruapan.

Tzararacua waterfall near
the city of Uruapan.

in the same park.

In 1943, Paricutin volcano produced its first eruption.
There are now tourist routes for off-road vehicles,
pathways for hikers and horses available for hire for
any visitors wishing to explore the lava fields and the
recovering woodland, climb the crater or visit the
remains of Parangaricutiro church.

Following pages and end:
Paricutin, the volcano that first erupted in 1943 before the
gaze of the p'urhépecha farmer Dionisio Pulido.

Vasco de Quiroga's testament lives on thanks to the purépechas. The Vasco de Quiroga Route will be highly appreciated by travellers who will be able to enjoy, during the entire year, wonderful sunshine and enjoyed the refreshing rain.

Michoacán is the best place for cultural tourism, it is a kind of university to enable tourists to return to their homes knowing a little more about what the world is, thanks to the work of a learned man who is deserving of all recognition.

Miguel de la Quadra.

Miguel de la Quadra.

Bell towers of Parangaricutiro,
the survivors of the lava
from Paricutin.

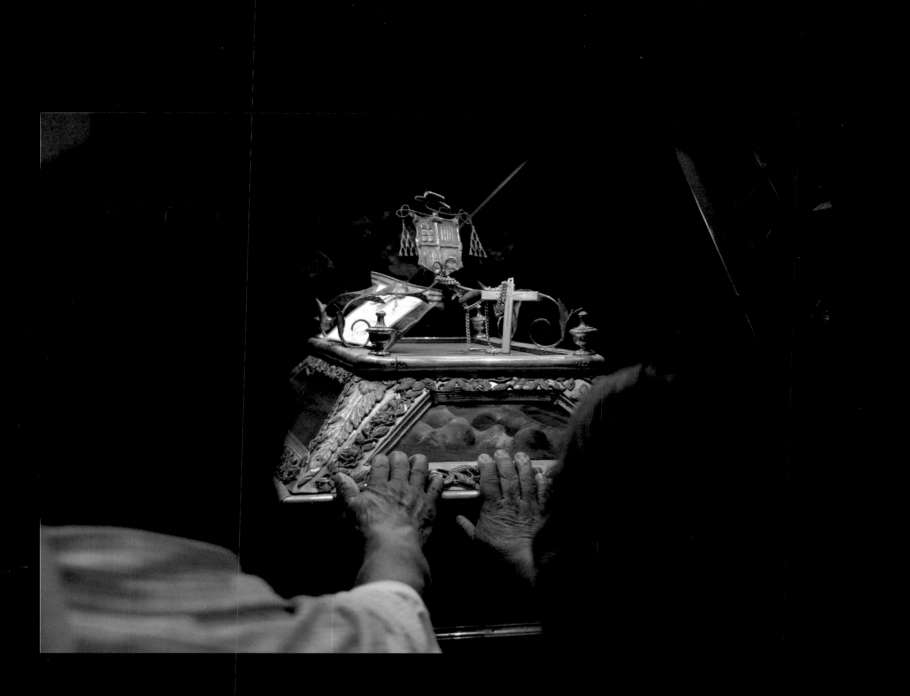

While I live I will nourish my lambs, I will work until I die and I will voluntarily give my life for them.
VASCO DE QUIROGA.
Testament.

Our commitment — we, the young indigenous people — is to recreate our culture, just as Vasco de Quiroga did in his time, transmitting it vigorously, developing it and taking from the modern age what we need, so that this culture does not end, but that it has the same capacity as other cultures, faithfully following the path of our ancestors.

María Guadalupe Hernández Dimas